This book is dedicated to my father and mother, Herbie and Mina – who care for me and who care about me.

Contents

Foreword

Bill lives with his thoughts like the Biblical Zacchaeus, atop an invading sycamore branch. He is a holy delightful writer. He dreams about learning everything on this playground of the earthen creation. He is a teacher who listens, lectures and inspires. He is vision for the wanting and wasting, hearing for the learning impaired, and all served with a razor commentary in gravelly tones of rightness and truth.

Bill is called, for truth to spread and breathe healing balm landing smack on the fractured thought of others. He hopes to influence a revival melody for many, but many more for the journey to mental health.

Bill consistently and often writes his poetry in three sentence pieces of irony. His poems are sublimely different than the short order expression from a three line Japanese Haiku or a Hebrew poem built on similar, side by side, parallel verses. This is not a critique of the quality of the different kinds of poems but a listing of subtle differences out here.

His initial line tells a brief story of what exists on his footpath for change. The second line carries a nugget of truth and recommends a last sentence of collision and conclusion looking for an answer in a convicting target. We are repeatedly showered with suggestion, implicitness, subtlety, and expressions of heavy and hard truth. All three progressive lines delve out true truth, and not the old standby of love and beauty.

Bill drains his concluding sentences mightily in three short lines always asking the reader of the world, 'isn't your answer worse than what you started with and farther away than where we should go?' The pain and conviction lies in being shown by the author what we might already know up in the sycamore tree.

We can only nervously laugh in response, glad that we are not the bull's eye of an excellent arrowsmith.

Who offers the arrow
Pierces to know us.

I met Bill McKnight when I moved to Belfast in 2008 to do faith-based volunteer work, and we have become very good mates. We are drawn together by our interest in writing and reciting poetry and by our Christian faith. More than this I appear to lack physical health and I can depend on Bill to show up. He encourages my writing. Bill says he lacks mental health and he can confide in me. I encourage his confidence. We are just two fellows who were providently drawn together to banish our fears and build our friendship.

Congratulations on publishing your poems Bill.

Ward Stothers
Belfast 2012

Acknowledgements

Mr Wesley McGrath and family

Mr David Boyd and family

Mrs Rhoda Noble (Belfast Royal Academy)

Mr Thomas E Forbes (Belfast City Missionary)

Staff in psychiatric services, Belfast

Dr Wesley Rainey, GP

Rev Robin Harris and Mrs Sandra Harris

Rev Norman Hamilton O.B.E. and Mrs Evelyn Hamilton

Mr Michael Harrison (Hewitt and Gilpin Solicitors, Belfast)

Jim (Stacks Bookshop, Belfast)

Kathy Harris; Stephen McAree; Andrew Brownlee

Introduction

Bill McKnight wrote to me about five years ago. I had just published a book about stigma, discrimination and mental health, and he sent me a few poems to read. He attached a short message saying that I might be interested to read them. I was startled by their force. Since then we have kept in touch and from time to time I am moved, and often inspired, when he sends me a few more poems.

Writing poetry came relatively late for Bill, as he says 'at 40 discovered I have a brain'. He has a remarkable and spare style that cuts to the quick of his subject matter: surviving with mental illness. These messages are by turn distressing or humorous or affirming, but are never sentimental. He simply expresses his experience in remarkably distilled form. He speaks of the isolation and loneliness that can be a part of mental illness, sometimes from a simultaneous avoidance of others, who also tend to uncomfortably withdraw. He poignantly parodies the common stock phrases that others use, intended to be comforting but experienced as profoundly beside the point. He softly speaks of the ill lit area between the public front of 'normality' and the back story of the real sense of self, which can feel like a 'meltdown of the heart and mind'.

These poems are sometimes brutally honest, and the writer admits that 'reality comes at a cost'. But ultimately these poems are testimony both to Bill's great artistic skill and also his fundamental optimism (compare the first and second version of 'Friends'). Bill's readers are now fortunate that he has conquered his self-consciousness and allowed this volume to be published, in defiance of the forces of stigma: 'I refuse to wear this so-called disgrace'.

Graham Thornicroft
Professor of Community Psychiatry
King's College London, Institute of Psychiatry
April 2012

LOUD SILENCE

positive thinking (gone pear-shaped)

I'm beautiful.
I'm clever.
I'm able.
I'm talented.
I'm witty.
I'm great.
Gee. I'm a pain!

mental illness (a glimpse)

Mental illness,
what is it like?
Ever been self-conscious?
How do I appear?
I rub my nose;
I look at the toes
of my shoes.
Should I look to the right?
Should I look to the left?
Should I look up, down, around?
Perhaps a little too hot under the collar?
Perhaps a little redder in the cheek?
Perhaps a little too casual?
Perhaps a little too neat?
Is my voice too loud?
Is my voice too soft?
Am I being over-heard?
Perhaps a little too … everything!
Mental illness
is like self-consciousness,
only worse.
And self-consciousness
is like
hell.

Friends

They don't call me sad.
They don't call me bad.
They don't call me mad.
They don't call me.

Riddle

I wanna get rich –
you'll know who I am.
I wanna get marketed –
you'll know who I am.
I wanna get in with the in-crowd –
you'll know who I am.
I wanna get famous –
you'll know who I am.
Who am I?

Making life easier?

Hot water on tap.
Electric lights.
And indoor loos.
Fridges.
Freezers.
Central heating.
Package tours too ...
making life easier?
But life is tough.
The cracks are appearing.
We cannot cope.
So many people
at the end of their ...
r
o
p
e

suicide

"I've got to be strong."
"I've got to be strong."
"I've got to be strong."
Now he's gone.
Was his strength 'put on'?

Comfort zone

I don't want
to get involved with you –
you who are weak and upset.
Because you might upset me.

Jim'll fix it

Face up to your ghosts.

yes, but …

Put the past behind you.

yes, but …

Be strong.

yes, but …

Be in control.

yes, but …

You need to manage your feelings.

yes, but …

Time is a great healer.

yes, but …

Pull yourself together.

yes, but …

You'll get over it.

yes, but you're not listening.

Mentally ill (but not stupid)

Squirrel Nutkin's schizophrenic.
Some people say she's bonkers.
But Squirrel Nutkin differentiates
'tween hazelnuts and conkers!

Mountain summit

It is too frightening to make a mistake.
And the mountain ahead is so high.
It is too frightening to say what I think.
And the mountain ahead is so high.
It is too frightening to let my anger out.
And the mountain ahead is so high.
It is too frightening to trust.
And the mountain ahead is so high.
It is too frightening to take a risk.
And the mountain ahead is so high.
It is too frightening to love.
And the mountain ahead is so high.
It is too frightening to live.
And the mountain ahead is so high.
Aaargh!! It's too frightening to be frightened.
And the valley below
is splendid to the eye.

Schizo-affective disorder

Depression is out-dated
when I feel elated!
Elation is out-dated
when I feel deflated!

Front versus up-front

Lee is imprisoned
by what '*they*' might see.
So Lee is busy hiding Lee.
Liz is free.
Liz
just
is.

Hope

It is said that the darkest hour
is just before dawn.
In a similar vein
growth and change
can be gained
at the moment of greatest pain.

Loud silence

Withdrawn from society.

There's stigma.

There's secrecy.

There's shame.

And the service-user's pain.

Loud silence is often the voice

of the voiceless 'insane'.

Acute illness

mental gridlock.

fear like buckshot.

emotional shellshock.

meltdown of the heart and mind.

all pain.

no gain.

insane?

At the hairdresser's

"How are you, Bill?" she asked.
"I'm a bit depressed," I replied.

"My sister gets depressed;
I must be the *strong one*," she said.

Her razor cut my hair.
Her tongue cut my feelings.

Dr. Who?

I disclose to you. You don't disclose to me.
In this power imbalance lies an inequality.
Dr. Who, if such a relationship is to your credit
I simply don't get it! Unfairapeutic!

good mood

The rain is away.
It's a wonderful day!

Rather dead than Fred?

He lives
in a very frightening world;
it's mostly inside his head.
Some people call him 'a nutter';
family call him 'our Fred'.

Schizo-mania

Schizos!
Look around your town.
They're the ones
buried above ground.

Zombies!
In your main street they are found.
They're the ones
buried above ground.

Down and outs!
Dressed 'down'.
They're the ones
buried above ground.

Mrs. Smith. Mr. Brown.
They're the ones
who bury us
above ground.

The Daily Gob

The tabloid heading reads:
"Schizo kills pensioner",
and makes no mention of the 99.9%
of normal murderers.

The mental health professional

Does she really care?
With one eye on me
and one eye on her career.

What's the point?

All the world's a stage.
Pretenders on parade.
A poet's been gleaning:
Security.
Belonging.
Meaning.
And what's his epic tale?
Real life is to be real.

World Mental Health Day

"Mental illness – raising awareness.
Do you get it?"

"I'm afraid I'll get it from you!"

Burning the midnight oil (on my P.C.)

I stay up all night
'cos sleeping dogs don't bite.
I sleep all day,
afraid of the affray.

Duh!

I was insane.
But at forty
discovered
I have a brain!

Fear

Fear.
Interferes.

Flexi-'bill'-ity!

When the breakdown came
I was much too brittle.
When the next wind blows
I will bend a little!

Friends

They don't call me sad.
They don't call me bad.
They don't call me mad.
They don't call me.
I know! I'll be a friend.
I'll call them!

Labelled by you

I wear a subtle tattoo.
Its name is 'taboo'.
Worried you'll be branded too?

Mental anguish

I'm sick of being sick.
And heroin's not the trick.
Indeed, there is no easy fix.

Mental health problem?

He's on 'his knees'
and he's feeling unease
'cos he's failing to please.
Is this behavioural
or is this disease?

Mind's eye

Doctor, my mind is out of focus.
Like wearing glasses
that have a wrong prescription.
Will medication mend the blur
and give me back my vision?

Reality for sale?

How can I know reality
if I'm unwilling to be real.
And reality is not purchased
in a Summer sale.
Reality comes at a cost –
dearer but better than anything bought.

There's a fine line between …

A scribble!
Should it be scrubbed out?
Rubbed out?
Straightened out?
Or remain a little bit messy?
Madness or creativity?

Fear

If I'm a success	I'll handle it.
If I fail	I'll handle it.
If I'm pressured	I'll handle it.
If I become unemployed	I'll handle it.
If my business grows	I'll handle it.
If my spouse leaves me	I'll handle it.
Fear	I'll handle it?

Hope?

The show must go on!
Must it?

Laughter

I told a doctor,
"The seagulls are laughing at me."
The doctor laughed, too!
(Who says laughter
is the best medicine!)

Mad man

I met a man
who thinks he is
high king of Ireland.
His rival is
the grand old duke of York
who's bought a 'des res'
south of Cork!

Self

I'm the king
of my castle
and I am thoroughly
miserable!

The man who ran away from himself

Mental illness was a
certainty though few saw
it coming. The man in
question was running away
from himself. When the
running ceased the pain
began de-numbing him. Sobering.
What can I say? An
exposé of one man's lunacy.
Now, having turned, he is
running in the opposite way.

Terminology?

Schizophrenia
may not be an illness.
Nonetheless, for many
it's a life term.

Depression

Having suffered
I felt cleansed.
Then I'd cut
myself emotionally
and suffer
all over again …

Sticks and stones

Sticks and stones may break my bones
but stigma really hurts me.

Stigmattack

I refuse to wear
this so-called disgrace
shame-faced.
My stance is plain –
no longer will you shame me
with a name.

Stigmafraid

Stigmafraid?
Struth!
Who's afraid
of the big bad wolf?

Recovery

Depression's lifting.
'tis music to my ears.
I heard a smile today!
An unchained melody.

Developments?

Pooh sticks.
Chop sticks.
But nothing sticks
like stigma.

To hell and back

a   to   b   via   'z'.

Recovery

Wellness –
living with illness.

Stigma

Insight
that is skin-deep.

CPSIA information can be obtained at www.ICGtesting.com
Printed in the USA
LVOW11s1841080616

491761LV00002B/360/P